Nothing But Happiness

By: Brandon King

ISBN: 978-1-365-84268-9 **Printed Format**

TABLE OF CONTENTS

The chapters draw you in to make you sit back and take a second look at your life. This book teaches you no matter what you've been through or where you are in your life, you can always become a happy you. This book is truly inspiring!

- RM

This book is a stepping stone to finding true happiness.

- ID

This book is honest and devoted to help its readers. I'm glad to have read a book that incorporates a sense of uniqueness and truth.

- VH

This book is personal, but understandable, and relatable. It has made me think of things I went through and how I found my happiness, my strengths, and the fighter within. I am happy where I am in life, but with this book, I know I can be happier with simple steps. Thank you for sharing your experience and making me realize things I didn't notice before. You are an inspiration. You are a gift from God. You are someone who has made an impact on my life. You are a blessing. This book is a must read!

- JG

FOREWORD

When I was given the opportunity to write the foreword for *Nothing But Happiness*, it sounds cliché but I was happy. Knowing that my best friend had stepped out and decided to share his story to the world of what he has overcome in his life was not only bold, but it was encouraging. At some point in our lives, we all have been depressed, angry, or frustrated in our current situations. All of us are also guilty in searching for happiness whether it's through money, sex, drugs, or anything that can fill the void for the moment. Once you get to the point in life where you know that true happiness comes from above and within, then and only then, will you be able to transform your life to a more positive outlook.

My brother has finally found where his happiness stems from. After reading this book, I pray you do as well!

-    RG

PREFACE

Every person has their own story and this is no different. The book you are holding in your hands is my voice. I decided to put my experiences out into the world, specifically dealing with my parents' divorce back in 2009. At that time, my life was filled with depression, anger, resentment, and frustration. I couldn't understand why my happiness was so greatly affected by them, but I figured it out. Currently, I'm still dealing with the divorce, however presently; I'm in the stage of contentment. With the assistance of my Christian faith, self-confidence, and trusting the process, I have no complaints of what I've experienced during those rough times. Today, I am satisfied with life.

The purpose of this book is to encourage you to open up your mind, to trust yourself, and to help you discover your path to maintain your daily positivity. Expand your countless possibilities of living the positive life you always wanted to live, to learn healthier habits, and to explore different aspects about yourself. My goal for you is to ALWAYS acknowledge your happiness because it is important.

Throughout the book, you will read the chapters which are strategically in chronological order to provide the steps in what I believe will help you to achieve this. Although, I have not been through the worst circumstances in life, I've been through enough to hopefully build encouragement, motivation, and inspiration in you. Ultimately, I want you to consider this to be your "go to book" when you need some uplifting. Today, I want you to choose to be happy, and recognize you are responsible for your OWN happiness.

INTRODUCTION

What a roller coaster it has been these past few years since my parents' divorce. As I look back, my definition of happiness revolved around them. Over time, I had to grasp that happiness isn't meant to be surrounded by anything that can be stolen from you. We all will experience joyful moments but happiness is not just an emotion. This feeling will never stop, if you live every day in a positive way.

Life is tough and nowadays in our communities, workplaces, and school environments, you see all different types of emotions varying from depression, anger, nervousness, fear, anxiety, and so on. Yet still, achieving happiness is so important to understand because it's vital for our health. I believe happiness is the best satisfaction in the entire world, but the toughest emotion to maintain. If you are not experiencing this joy, I hope you will come to comprehend that you have what it takes to activate your happiness right now! I will assist in helping you shift your mindset to understand nothing should be put over your own happiness. Not your current job, the negativity in your life, the mistakes you've made, NOTHING. Sooner than later, I want this to stick into your brain as a mental reminder for you. Once you finish reading this book, my ambition is to have you progress into this lifestyle of maintaining happiness on your own. Have you ever heard the saying, practice what you preach? Preach the happiness you want for yourself into existence, and then practice this newer habit. You can achieve and be whoever, and whatever you put your mind to. It's up to you.

CHAPTER 1

TRANSFORM

It wasn't quite clear for me that I had to change my mind, in order for me to create the happiness I was looking for. I've realized our thoughts lead us to our behaviors, our behaviors leads to habits, and habits create our life. Even though, previously I had negative patterns, I am content with what I went through. Contentment isn't a matter of being joyful with everything going on in your life and never trying to live "perfectly." It's a matter of being satisfied with what you currently have, accepting what has happened, and realizing there is always room to improve.

If you're lacking this positivity, this can change by allowing yourself to transform your mind. Grasp right now, you have the ability to do this. Anything in your life can be different by renewing your mind. As you acknowledge your negative thoughts, you can accept the positive ones to come in. By doing, it will produce positive results, habits, and a mindset.

I'm aware there are numerous emotions we feel every day that are triggered by our mind. Depending on the circumstance, when we experience something negative or positive, it causes us to react in a certain way. As well as, the people we surround ourselves with, our past or present situations, can potentially affect our personalities, mannerisms, and standards. I want to tell you whatever emotion you are currently feeling at this moment; you have the ability to transform it. You may feel unhappy now, but you have the ability to convert it into happiness. You may be fearful, but you have the capacity to transform that into feeling confident. The list can go on, but your present emotion can be changed. This capability of mind transformation is not a superhuman power; it is more so on activating your willpower. The secret is to reconstruct your thought process by understanding your life can be shifted, if you think differently. If you control your negative thinking, you can rewire your brain to think positively which I like to call your mind tool. I know it's easier said than done but I believe this mind tool transformation will help you think wiser, become more conscious of your actions, and become a more positive person by not allowing the negativity affect you. You must realize it is impossible to change the world around you, but you control what affects you.

I want to tell you this renewal will not be done overnight, which is why I repeat—it's not a superhuman power. All of us are uniquely different in our own way; we have different mindsets, and experience different life events every day. I can't preach, "Just be happy 24/7 and don't stress, or be upset." That's impossible! No human being can achieve this and no one is perfect, because we aren't designed to be. It is okay to encounter and feel other emotions other than happiness because life isn't supposed to be flawless. But the good news is we all possess a powerful mechanism to change our state of mind to get rid of the negative thoughts and experiences that trigger another emotion other than happiness. The concept of mind transformation may seem difficult, but don't let it stop you because it didn't stop me! Ever since I started controlling my thought process, the circumstances and the people who once had an influence on me, didn't receive the same response. Reason being, I'm not the former person I used to be.

The Old Me

Negative, scared, and hidden. Three words that controlled me, and held me captive. I submitted my personal statement to Montclair State University, but I knew deep down I rushed the process. I wasn't focused on this statement; rather my parents' lack of communication was getting the best of me. To put the cherry on top, I had a score of 1080 on my SATs and an 18 on my ACTs. I knew these scores would affect my acceptance but I didn't care. Due to my paranoia, I decided to schedule a meeting with my guidance counselor to talk about my college process.

I arrived to her office, sat down, and handed my statement to her. In a matter of minutes, she scanned through it, frowned and responded, "Oh I see why you didn't get in to that school." I was in shock when I heard this. I felt as if she slapped me across the face. She crushed my hopes, dreams, and any motivation to pursue this college. I didn't know what to say, so I thanked her for her time and walked out of her office politely. As I was pacing towards my locker, I realized she didn't care about my future or me personally. Ironically, there was no guidance, encouragement, or counseling I received from that meeting. Sadly, what she failed to see was a frustrated, lost student trying to succeed in life. She didn't even believe in me. I had something to prove to her but most importantly to myself.

As a child of divorced parents', lonely in a world full of brokenness, my biggest challenge was how to be happy during this rough period. Before their divorce, I used to love arriving home to be in their presence. I enjoyed our family gatherings, holidays, driving in one car as a family, and saying good night to both of them at the same time. In my eyes, I felt the love was in the air.

When I reached my junior year of high school, I noticed a change in my parent's relationship. I didn't see them interact as a couple as often as I used to. Their communication was lacking and it got to the point where my father slept downstairs. In my mind, I thought having space between them was "healthy." My judgement wasn't correct and as days passed by, things suddenly changed for the worst. Their affection towards one another disappeared, and their anger towards one another grew. At that moment in time, I couldn't understand how fast love could turn into resentment. As the disagreements continued, it took a toll on our family.

I remember the night I prayed to God asking for them to be separated. I was tired of hearing them fighting and yelling. Then a couple of weeks passed by and in a blink of an eye, it seemed like my prayer was answered. "Your father and I are getting a divorce" is what my mother told me. Tears were rolling down my face like a river. I couldn't believe my prayer came true because I didn't mean to ask for this to happen. I started to question myself; who could I look up to as an example for my future relationship? Who could I ask for advice? As their child, I looked up to them to hold us together when things went south. I couldn't handle the reality of the news. This made me become fearful and I gave up on my own happiness since it revolved around them.

As days continued on, I just couldn't grasp what would become my reality. I felt like I was still in a dream hoping for someone to wake me up. My family was being destroyed right in front of my eyes and I had no control over it. With the thought of my parents' remarrying another person, I wanted to let them know how I felt about this. I took the initiative to write them both a letter expressing my feelings about having a step-parent. This idea didn't sit well with me, and then suddenly, my mindset switched to rage. I wasn't diagnosed with depression but there was a point where I felt numb. There were days where I cried to myself thinking about all the changes that would soon take place. Not living together, family pictures, my future marriage, or being with each other on holidays. And most importantly, knowing when I went to sleep at night I would wake up to both of them not there. I thought my life couldn't get any worse.

It was tough for me to believe there was ONE person who could understand or sympathize, to what I was going through. I questioned myself and God as to why did I deserve this? What did I do wrong? Why me? It took me years to search for an answer. Then, it hit me. I realized there isn't an explanation to any of these questions. They can only be answered through experience and time; some questions will always stay unanswered. Through my faith, God knew what he was doing in my life to prepare me for the future. He knew what I needed to go through in order to mold me into the person I am today. Without these experiences, I wouldn't have learned what I am capable of handling.

Now I understand, everyone has gone through different experiences, or has encountered something far worse than what I experienced. Some experiences are filled with darkness: sexual, physical or emotional abuse, severe depression, family death and so on. While others experience the light: loving families, an unforgettable childhood, and a positive environment and so on. But I feel most experiences are filled with a mixture of the light and darkness. Regardless of how much you've endured, good or bad, you can't change what has happened. Realize, the circumstances that are meant to break you down can only build you up.

At some point, we all will suffer, run into obstacles, and experience pain. I understand these circumstances are traumatic and can leave you feeling hopeless, but don't allow it. During this evolution, the beginning is always rough. But whatever you are going through right now is helping you become a courageous individual. This is why it is highly important for you to learn to transform your mind because it can improve your life tremendously. You'll start to be able to work with the same types of challenges that used to cause you such frustration, agony, and suffering, which will change to a consistent level of calm, joy, optimism, and trust.

I encourage you to NEVER put yourself down from your past or current negative experiences. This will only cause your self-esteem or confidence to diminish. There is no reason to bully yourself because it takes time for where you want to be in life. You can't avoid these encounters because these aspects are a part of life. Even through adversity, the best news is everything will eventually repair itself. Our hearts, minds, souls, and bodies will heal through time. Just have confidence that your wounds will restore and don't ever think your happiness won't come back because it will!

The New Me

After my parent's divorce I can truly say, my life has turned around for the better. Through the years, this mind transformation became possible with the assistance of prayer, patience, acceptance, and forgiveness. Everything I have been through has shown me how to be a better person of improvement. I am more confident, mature, and a brave individual who is ready to continue this adventure of life. I want you to become this person as well. Be conscious of this; we can't prepare for the next negative thing to happen in our lives. If we could, we probably wouldn't live life for ourselves because we would be so cautious about what is going on around us. Regardless, this is why mistakes and failures are important. These factors are a part of your learning process. Every time you experience a bad circumstance, you learn a lesson. This is a great way to prepare you for a brighter future and improve the person you are destined to be. Another incentive is once you know better; you'll do better for yourself, and have better preparation on how to handle any situation.

I can honestly say there is no "perfect" time when you will decide to renew your mindset. Understand it is okay to not be aware, however become conscious of the more you continue to keep the same negative mindset, the less opportunities it will give you to enjoy moments of your life. If you're tired of the way negativity is taking control of your life, you have the ability to transform it because YOU ARE RESPONSIBLE FOR YOUR OWN HAPPINESS. Make the decision to change today! Decide to shift your thought process by not allowing the negativity trigger you. If you want to achieve the happiness you desire, you must choose happiness first. Then, go after it by creating the path towards what makes you happy. Find peace through faith, go out and experience life. Go dance, go sing, and do whatever it is that will keep you smiling.

I hope you are encouraged by what you have read. For those who have currently or dealt with their parents' divorce, I hope this motivates you to stay strong. I want you to understand you have two options in life: you can decide to let what you are going through to shape you negatively or you can learn to become wiser and a tougher individual. Either one, I would hope you would want to learn and take the positive route to change your mind to become stronger. Again, I will repeat, none of this is an overnight process. This is a transformation and an educated evolution of yourself. IT IS NOT AN UNREACHABLE GOAL EITHER! NO EXCUSES! If you're not happy right now, would you like to be?

Once, I was able to attack my negative mindset, life became so much clearer. I hope I ignited the fire in you to stimulate your mind to change or you can let this information go through one ear and out the other. Ultimately, it's up to you to decide whether you take the first steps of transformation. *Nothing But Happiness.*

"Progress is impossible without change, and those who cannot change their minds cannot change anything."
George Bernard Shaw

"Everyone wants to live on top of the mountain, but all the happiness & growth occurs while you're climbing it."
Andy Rooney

"I'm trying to free your mind, Neo. But I can only show you the door. You're the one that has to walk through it."
Morpheus

"If you will transform your mind, God will transform your life."
Joel Osteen

"If you can change your mind, you can change your life."
William James

"Change your thoughts and you change your world."
Norman Vincent Peale

CHAPTER 2

CONCENTRATE

Concentration is the mind's ability to focus on something with ALL of your attention. To be able to concentrate is a skill, NOT a gift. It is not about having an IQ of Albert Einstein or having a prodigy type of memory. It is about how focused your interest is in something, and giving yourself more time to intensify your desires on what you want to succeed in. If your focal point isn't on your happiness, you can change this.

Even though the ability to focus on one thing is tough while balancing your priorities in your life, you must train your mind to concentrate. This discipline will help you tune in to the transformation of your mind. You'll be able focus on what you want to achieve in your life, your happiness, and surrounding yourself with the right people, which will hopefully bring you positive energy. Unfortunately, concentrating on positivity is difficult because we will always experience some kind of stress. However, it is not impossible to focus effectively on the essential aspects that are healthy for us. I want you to understand this concept is a serious matter. Right now, you need to search for the important things to center on. Such as, your happiness, family, career goals, and positivity, and then avoid the distractions in your life like negative people, environments, and your mindset.

This mental skill can develop numerous opportunities for you by sharpening your focus, gain inner peace, and assist the success rate on what you want to accomplish. These are just some benefits but realize your mind will become stronger. It will obey you more, not engage in fear, negative thoughts, or overthinking. Without targeting your focus on your happiness, the mind will jump all over the place causing distractions to enter. Nonetheless, you are never too occupied to focus on your concentration. There is no excuse about not having the "time" to do this. You must practice this powerful development because it will help you in the near future. This is a commitment you deserve to yourself to understand your **MIND**.

MIND

Better concentration and focus has made my life easier, less complicated, and more productive. If you want to understand why concentration is so important, I took the time to create an acronym that will hopefully help you understand the importance of concentrating on what you want in your life. Each letter has a significant meaning to it which I've observed throughout my life. Here are the key steps I've identified to comprehend your **MIND**.

M stands for *making* a decision to concentrate. I like to think of this concept as to focus on positivity. At any given time, if I experienced something negative, I concentrated more on the positive outcome. I had to push out all the feelings that weren't positive so I could achieve this. When I encountered a gloomy person or situation; I always asked myself, "What did I learn?" If I learned something, I took the lesson into consideration, and moved on. By understanding this, has helped me build my mental strength when facing stress. I want you to know there's no need to dwell in your past negative experiences because you can't change them. Continue to learn and focus on your happy moments.

I stands for *ignore* the negativity in your life. It sounds easier said than done, but this is not impossible to do. After a while, once you dominate your mind to tune in to positivity, you will not be disturbed by the negativity. If you ignore negativity, the things or people who caused you to react in the wrong way, will not get the same reaction anymore. Furthermore, later in the book, I will discuss about two types of people, and how we socialize with them. You must decide how you will manage your time with these people in your life. I believe getting rid and avoiding these distractions will help keep your mind in a focused position. Remember, miserable people always love company!

N stands for *non-resistance* to change. I started to shift my mind, my attitude, and my character by not being afraid of change. I fell in love with the new development of my self-growth. I stopped pointing my fingers at my parents' for my depression because I knew it wasn't their fault. My attitude was poor so I had to accept myself unconditionally and get out of my comfort zone. I had to understand, change comes from getting out of your comfort zone. There is no room for growth if you are stuck in a place that you are "comfortable" in. I understand diving into the unknowns can be fearful. It can potentially bring up plenty of questions. But sometimes you have to leave what is familiar in order to explore the unfamiliar to discover a better you. You will never know what you are capable, what you can manage, and who or what is stopping you, if you don't step out of your comfort zone. I encourage you to step out your comfort zone with confidence. You won't regret it!

D is to *dominate* your emotions to give yourself the ability to concentrate. I felt like there was nothing I could do about the stress in my life. The pressure of working a job, getting ready for college, negative people, and thinking of what's next in my life, put a lot of weight on my shoulders. But I realized, stress management is doable by using my faith and taking it one day at a time. We can't ever limit ourselves and tell ourselves we can't do something. If anything, we have to change our negative vocabulary words because we'll start to believe them. Just like in any sport competition, the winning team dominates their opponent. You can control your fears and the things that are holding you back to achieve happiness. The good news is concentration is the key to achieve this. Remind yourself to never give up because this comes with practice. Don't be afraid to fail because it's part of your growth. Once you get comfortable with focusing on what's important, then you'll have dominant results.

I hope this acronym will make sense to you and make it easier to comprehend your mind. As I applied this acronym to myself, you can make this lifestyle change too, by applying MIND to your life experiences. Each letter is a daily commitment to practice but don't let the process stop you. It's all up to you to control it, and use towards your success.

For You and Against You

Throughout your life, you may notice that some days go the way you want it to, and some days don't. I will like to call these two different types of days, "for you" and "against you". The for you type of day, also known as a good day, is a day that gives you extreme joy, and keeps getting better by the minute. These are the days that present no type of obstacles to get through. The against you type of day, also known as a bad day, will give you stress and frustration. These are the days where life smacks you across the face. Think for a moment the last time you had a bad day and a good day. What were your feelings? What were you concentrated on?

So, why the emphasis on the good and bad days? Well, for starters the determining factor to your good and bad days is how you approach them. Often times, we don't determine what makes a bad day really a horrible day, or what makes a good day really a perfect day. I like to believe it is simply our expectations and perspectives. I want you to start realizing this too. We can't avoid stress but we can effectively manage it by understanding, the repercussions of our expectations and perspectives.

First, let's talk about expectations. I believe this is the **number one disappointment** in our lives. We pick on ourselves and people when they don't meet our own expectations. We expect people to not disappoint us or treat us a certain way. Even during a normal day, when we predict bad things to happen, we'll most likely end up in an "against you" type of day. On the positive side, if you assume good things to happen, then you'll most likely end up in a "for you" kind of day. Take note, the more we lessen our expectations, the lesser opportunities it'll give us to say, "I expected this anyway." If we could just stop having these unrealistic expectations, it would save ourselves a lot of unhappy moments!

Second, perception is everything. Each one of us wear different perspective lenses through which we view the world. The way you perceive people, your environment, the way you see life, is ultimately how everything will play out in your life. Once you understand this, it will be much easier for you to respect others and the ways in which they view life. Some of us experience similar situations and some of us can't even relate. Either way, by concentrating what is going on in a positive sense, instead of the negative, it will put you in a better position to have your happiness come into existence.

Keep in mind with encountering these types of days develops memories. We all can agree, bad flashbacks are a lot easier to recall than the good ones. We remember the people that left our lives on rough terms, regretful memories, and emotions words can't express. While all of these are a part of life, your negative days are the memories we have to concentrate on. There is a unique connection with our emotional health and our daily lifestyle. If you continue to carry the hurt with you all day long, this will give you an unhealthy lifestyle. Right now, I want to encourage you to detach yourself from anything that doesn't allow you to concentrate on your happiness. Once my parents got divorced, it was difficult to transition.

"Hey Brandon, can you and Jay meet me at Suvio's after school? I want to see you guys." said my mother. I responded,

"Yes, we want to see you too mom." After my parents' divorce, my brother and I moved in with our father. We haven't seen her in a couple of days since we moved out of our old house. It took a toll on both of us but the reality hit my mother pretty hard. As we arrived to the pizzeria, the atmosphere felt different. My mother's energy was a little off and I knew she was worried about us, just like any parent. After we ordered pizza, we sat down at the table and I glanced at her face. Once we began to eat, her eyes filled up like fountains with tears streaming down her cheeks. She was so wounded at the circumstance of not seeing her kids daily. Although this affected my brother and I seeing my mom like this, I knew one day, we all would be stronger in due time.

Even though I can recall tons of bad days, I can replay this hurtful memory like if it was yesterday. Until I realized, my brother and I will never go through this again. You have to understand, the worst memories are unhappy because you know they will never happen repeatedly. The main idea is that we have to go through the lowest of the low to appreciate the lessons that come after. We must never expect for the bad times to roll on forever. Without experiencing the horrible moments in our life, we wouldn't be grateful for the good ones.

I want to reassure you to not let your perspective and your expectations become dictators of your life. The truth is, being positive all day, every day is a relative concept. Honestly, it was very hard for me to always stay positive during my parents' divorce. Even with sharp focus and practice, I realized our emotions still go up and down like a seesaw. Regardless, if you are a master of positive thinking, you'll probably still have a few rocky moments here and there, and that's acceptable! Be appreciative of experiencing both of these two types of days and understand, not every day will go as planned. I've always believed sometimes we have to go through our worst days to receive our best days. Personally, I had to experience sadness to know what happiness is, which makes me humble from encountering these types of days.

Sooner or later, once you understand the concept of concentration, you'll create your own mental strength. It'll be easier for you to remain focus on what keeps you happy, be content with what you experience, and erase the negativity in your life. Whether you go through a "for you" or "against you" type of day, learn and grow with each choice you make. This will teach you how to properly prioritize the things that matter from the things that don't.

Too Much On My Plate

"I have way too much on my plate to even concentrate."

"I have more important things to concentrate on."

"I can't even think straight."

If you have thought about of any of these sayings before, then I hope you can understand what I was going through. Back then, I had my priorities mixed up because I was too focused on wrong things. My concentration wasn't on myself but everything around me.

While my parents were transitioning into their divorce, I had started my first job at Walgreens, finished up my sophomore year of high school, prepared myself for taking the SAT and ACTs, and started the process of applying to colleges. With all of these responsibilities, I felt like I had no time to breathe. It was an extraordinarily difficult time for me to even think about myself. I thought my priorities were manageable, but they weren't. There was a lot of pressure on my shoulders to prove to myself I was capable of handling all the pressure, but I couldn't. My plate was so bombarded which caused an enormous amount of distress.

As I look back, I failed to understand that I didn't put my own happiness on my plate. The stress followed me to school which led to my bad grades. Meanwhile, I had to prepare to apply to colleges which I wasn't too worried about. As a result of my laziness, I didn't get accepted into my top choice of college. My lack of effort in the SAT/ACT exams and my personal statement wasn't sufficient enough for the school to accept me. While of this was going on, it was a lot for me to handle the reality.

If you feel like you have a million things going on in your life and you have no time to think about yourself, think again. You make time for what is important to you. It can vary from having to go to school, career decisions to make, bills to pay, and children to feed, and so on. However, the main objective is to organize your plate with what's important to you. There could be some things you have on your plate that you no longer need. Such as other people's burdens, old memories, and emotions you can't let go of. Regardless, remember to not belittle yourself because you are not perfect. Just be cautious of not filling your plate with more than what you can eat. What I mean is, don't continue to take on more priorities than you can handle. Especially if you can't put your full concentration into each important responsibility you have. The grocery list you will potentially create will never be completed and will cause you to stress. As a result, you're more likely to give up on yourself because you won't be able to handle everything.

I want to assist you in prioritizing your plate by suggesting some steps that I anticipate will be helpful. First, take a deep breath. By closing your eyes and breathing will control your over-thinking. Then prioritize your plate by figuring out what are the most important items. Take out anything that doesn't belong on your plate and form healthier habits. Continue to concentrate on your productivity towards what you want to accomplish and make sure you have self-discipline with your new habits. Remind yourself what you allow on your plate will stay, if you don't acknowledge it is there, accept it, and act to change.

Triple Threat of A's

I will like to share with you my personal observations that have helped me seek a deeper insight of my inner feelings. There are three powerful words we must know to understand our emotions. I hope by making you aware of these words, will help you take action to change your circumstances.

I fell in love playing basketball ever since my mother taught me at a young age. As a beginner, learning the fundamentals were tricky, especially the triple threat. This is a basketball term

and feelings, without judgment; there is no wrong or right way to do this. Accept what has happened in your past or current situations. Act towards the renewal you want to see for yourself. Once, you think about the triple threat in relation to your life situation, I promise you the healing process will soon begin. Now, put those answers you have written down into action! Trust in your learning development because it's only beneficial for you. Continue to chip away at the layers we have so carefully built up to enable us to get to the root of the problems. Until then, our problems will continue.

Ms. Jennifer

Sooner than later, my close friends started noticing my parents weren't together. When they asked about my emotions towards the divorce, I didn't know how to respond. Honestly, I didn't want anyone to know how I was feeling, not to mention, what I was going through in my life. During this rough period, I was already feeling hopeless. I had a "whatever, it is what it is" type of mood when in reality, I was deeply broken. I then developed a wall higher than the Eiffel Tower to protect myself. As my wall went up, I thought no one could ever break it down... until I met Ms. Jennifer. She was my high school teen counselor in a program called Teen Pride. This program strived to help young individuals by providing free counseling to build up self-esteem, positivity, and healthy lifestyles. Amusingly, I was assigned to Ms. Jennifer by my high school guidance counselor. At first, I was skeptical because she was a stranger. I wasn't ready to deal with the reality of my problems. But I went with my gut and gave it a shot.

Occasionally, Ms. Jennifer and I would meet up during different class periods for an hour or so to talk. I remember the first time she came to my class. She approached the room very politely and asked my teacher if she could have a word with me. While I was walking out the class, I looked at the clock and saw I had 30 minutes left until it was over. I was excited because I was able to leave class early, but then my anxiety kicked in. This was our first meeting and I didn't know what to expect.

We conversed all the way to her office which wasn't a "normal" one. Due to limited space, her office was one of the locations where the school served breakfast. I thought this was strange but it was in a secluded area which made me feel comfortable. As I walked through the door, I saw other Teen Pride counselors inside. Ms. Jennifer introduced me to everyone and I politely said hello. After, we kept walking all the way to the back. Behind a piano, I saw two chairs so I assumed this was our destination. I looked around the room just to be aware of my surroundings. Then I sat down, looked at Ms. Jennifer, she gazed at me, smiled and politely asked, "So Brandon, tell me about yourself. How's life?"

Throughout the school year and our multiple sessions, I became more excited to see Ms. Jennifer. In the beginning of our meetings, I was terrified to open up to her. I questioned if she didn't know my story, then she wouldn't understand my pain. She would probably judge me and tell me something I wouldn't want to hear. But I asked myself, if she didn't know my journey, how can my wall be broken down? Well after hearing myself speak over and over again, my wall became smaller and smaller. It was tough for me, but she made it easy to express myself. She was empathetic, she understood everything I said, and she genuinely cared about my emotions. All in all, Ms. Jennifer was the sweetest, kindest, most caring person I have ever met in my life. She helped me acknowledge, accept, and act upon my inner feelings. This became a new self-discovery of myself and it opened the door for me to heal.

Too many times, when we express our feelings to someone, they speak before they listen. In reality, we rather have that person just listen to our stories instead of talking. I'm not suggesting you to seek professional advice, unless you feel comfortable, but we all have at least one person we feel satisfied enough to talk to. I suggest when you find the person you can open up to, *hear* yourself speak and acknowledge the emotions behind them. The reason why we don't acknowledge our feelings is because we choose not to talk about them. These unspoken words fly through our minds to the point where we feel like we're going crazy. But, these emotions can be released just by speaking about them. If you feel as if being silent and hidden will help solve your pain, you're wrong. It'll only cause more trouble to continue. But it's funny how the words, listen and silent are spelled with the same letters. This is why by listening to yourself speak will open up your silent emotions.

If you aren't acknowledging, accepting, or acting upon your current feelings, I believe you can change this. Keep in mind, there are two people you will deal with when expressing yourself: those who understand and those who don't. Either way, it's important to understand how YOU feel. No one can adjust how you feel, except yourself. Some days, you may have this self-negative conversation with yourself to convince you there's no one who will understand. Besides health professionals, there are people who will care about your story and will listen. Just be comfortable to opening up when you're ready. As well as be accepting of what you've been through because it was supposed to happen. Stop overthinking so much about why you don't have this or that, or what should have or could have been. Everything happens for a reason! I know it can be hard to accept the feelings from those horrible disappointments, the heated arguments, and those hurtful words you can't forget, but you have to try in order to remain at peace with yourself and the world. Just keep in mind, the more you hold your emotions in, the more of a ticking time bomb you will become. You don't ever want to let yourself explode, especially on the people you care about. As I said, my parents' divorce was a huge pill for me to swallow, but its examples like this that will make you into a better person. There are going to be some sunny days and rainy days, but God won't let the rain last forever. Keep your shield and armor on to continue the fight through the battle of life. Remember to tell yourself, *Nothing But Happiness*.

"The secret of concentration is the secret of self-discovery. You reach inside yourself to discover your personal resources, and what it takes to match them to the challenge."
Arnold Palmer

"There were two ways to be happy: improve your reality, or lower your expectations."
Jodi Picoult

"Concentration is the secret of strength."
Ralph Waldo Emerson

"This is why by listening to yourself speak will open up your silent emotions."
Brandon King

"Accept what is, let go of what was, and have faith in what will be."
Anonymous

CHAPTER 3
SEPARATE

As I was maturing through the years, I realized there was baggage I needed to separate myself from in order to remain positive. I wasn't ready for the change, but this is something I had to prepare for. I even noticed some things weren't just meant to be in my life. This included some adjustments of myself, people, places, and memories. I had to focus on my negative energy and the people I surrounded myself with. Once I mastered my focus on my concentration, the next thing to tackle off the list was separation. As my separation process continued, God opened new doors for me.

I highly encourage you to think about these components: the negativity in your life, your current environment, and the way you heal emotionally. All of these play a crucial role in your separation process. Mainly, you need to understand who and what is adding a positive meaning in your life and what aspects aren't adding any value to you. I believe you will not have a satisfying life, if you have an abundance of negativity around. If you continue to surround yourself with negativity, this will only distract you by disturbing your character from improving. You should continue to strive to be the best version of yourself. If you have the opportunity to detach yourself from any of these aspects, then do it. Lastly, realize where you are heading in life because some emotions, places, and people aren't meant to follow in the same direction. Just trust in this separation process.

The Separation Formula

What should I separate from in order to maintain my happiness? If you are thinking about this question, this can be filled in with numerous answers, but I found a simple equation to help you understand this. It goes as follows: **Life − Negative Habits = Separation.** You have one life to live, and one opportunity to make the most out of it. Although, you can't start your life over and make everything brand new, you can change anything you want right now. It is never too late! Lastly, there is no reason to settle for anything less than what you deserve. If you do decide to settle, realize you will enter your comfort zone and limit yourself. I understand it can be strange to explore something unfamiliar but realize if you dwell now, this can potentially become an unhealthy habit.

For my separation process, I had to get serious about my negative habits. I was telling myself, "I want to be happy. I want to change. I want to go back to the happy me." I wanted and wanted a lot of things to happen, but there was no action. I kept quiet about my feelings and stayed in my negative mindset. These negative mannerisms led me nowhere, but to a nonchalant attitude. Until after, I graduated high school, I made a New Year's resolution to myself. I wanted to figure out what I wanted in my life. But most importantly, I knew I didn't want to end up like my parents'. I wanted to do everything I could to not follow in their footsteps. Action was necessary so I had to discover healthier habits. This included transforming my poor mindset to positivity, talk about what I was going through with Ms. Jennifer, organize my priorities, and continued to pray. This transformation continued by separating myself from anything that didn't add value to my life. This included my loser type of people, negative emotions, and memories. Now understand, your separation process will be different than mine and it will not be simple. You'll have a lot of questions towards yourself during this process, which will spark this learning renewal. It should be encouraging to know, you will discover a brighter path towards a newer you. I trust you can apply this equation because I have confidence this will help.

To repeat the steps, you must look at your life right now. If there are no positive habits, feed yourself these nutrients and then get rid of the negative ones. Lastly, be honest and open with your heart on what you need to detach from in order to achieve happiness. If you do not apply this formula, I believe you will not change anything around you. Take note, who you are surrounded with are the ones that are stopping you from doing anything you desire.

Your Winners and Losers

I assume we all struggle, or have struggled, with an identity crisis. We tried to be someone we weren't just to fit in with someone or a group of people. We gossiped with others, we compared ourselves, but what does that solve? Isn't it funny, the more you tried, the more you realized that you didn't fit in? k"fitting in" is an illusion. Life is hard when you don't know who you are, but do not allow people, your environment, and your circumstances mold you into someone you are not meant to be.

Growing up, I always wanted to be the most popular kid in high school that everyone enjoyed being around. I wanted the attention of others since I wasn't getting any at home. Ironically, since I am an identical twin, I was that "cool kid." When I was younger, I had two types of friends, the people that I could cause trouble with and the people who were too good for trouble. As I matured, I realized I wasn't being myself. I was so worried about "fitting in" with everyone, when in reality, all I had to be was myself and people would accept me for who I am. If you are dealing with the same type of situation of trying to get acceptance from others, I encourage you to stop! Instead, continue to be the uncommon human being you are meant to be and everyone will welcome you for who you are.

Nowadays we don't realize our surroundings due to our social norm. We are comfortable with people that act and think the same way as we do. I was told by someone, "We are the average of the five people we spend time with daily." Right now, I encourage you to think about your friends, family, coworkers, and acquaintances. Reason being is because there are certain people you do not need to surround your energy with. What do I mean by this? I like to categorize these two types of people as winners and losers. To make it clearer, think of the people who are positive and negative in your life.

First let's start off with the winners. This type of person can be our family members, closest friends, and coworkers that are in our lives. These type of people have been there for you when you needed them the most. They will encourage, strengthen, motivate, and keep you accountable for the things they want YOU to experience in life. Their energy is positive and can help encourage, or create your own energy to become more positive. Most importantly, the main responsibility of a winner is to help you **win**. Winning in your life, relationships, careers, school, successes, love, and the list can go on.

Here's what winner type of people would say to you:

"Great job, I hope you chase your dreams."

"Stay strong, you'll get through this."

"Hey, if you need anything, I'm always here for you, no matter what."

"I love you".

The list can go on with full of positive sayings. If you have winners in your life, continue to circle yourself with them because these are the people that want to see you prosper. Winner types of individuals want to see you happy! Being surrounded by them will clear away any negativity that exists around you, and create more space to welcome positivity in your life.

On the flip side, we all have experienced a person who is always negative. Their attitude stinks, their energy isn't always positive, and they try to bring down your mood. If a negative person is around you, realize they will feed you their negativity. These types of people can be in your family, friends, coworkers, and acquaintances. Try your best to concentrate on these harmful people. They'll suffocate you from your happiness because they want to see you fail. Their main responsibility is to assist in losing yourself in the process of your self-development, stop you from achieving your dreams, help create a negative mindset, and crush your positive spirits. The reason why losers act this way is because they focus on what's missing in their lives. Take a moment to think about this person or people in your life.

Here's what negative comments you would hear from a loser type of person:

"You can't do anything."

"You need to grow up."

"You think you are better than me?"

"You have to change."

There is more negative criticism but notice how every sentence starts with YOU...YOU...YOU...YOU. A loser type of person will make you think YOU are the one who needs the help, but in reality, it is he or she who needs the guidance. This person will try to mold you into something they don't see in themselves. Regardless, don't let their miserable attitude hinder yours, and don't let losers hold you back in life.

Currently, I have both winners and losers in my life. It doesn't cross my mind whether I want to "fit in" with people or worry about being accepted. I'm satisfied with the people who I can be myself around with. My father always told me, "Son never be a follower, always be a leader." I preach this saying to myself daily because I dared to be different. I don't need to follow any person that is not leading me into the direction into where I want to be in life. I've recognized if a loser type of person surrounds me, it doesn't make me one. The importance is setting boundaries with this type of person. I know who wants to continue to see the smile on my face, and those don't. I have to set the positive example and challenge myself to remain true to who I am because I am no better than them. We all aren't perfect, and don't have everything together in our lives, but we all have the capabilities of being in the winner category. We all can be winners if only we are willing to be one.

I hope you are thinking to yourself who is adding to your happiness, and those suffocating it. I can assume you are thinking of at least one person who's causing you this agony, or who has in the past. I can understand, reading this may be hard to completely cut off the loser type of people in your family, close friends, or coworkers. For some, it may be simple to trim people out of their life. But honestly, it's our comfort zones that make it so challenging for us. We get too comfortable with people who are stagnant which affects us later on in life. While, life doesn't work by allowing you to forget every person you know, you have to focus on yourself. This is all about how you handle being with your winners and losers. You can choose to stay positive being around negativity, or you can choose to be negative around positivity, this decision is up to you. Just remember, you need to understand your comfort zone.

The Butterfly Effect

I've noticed in life, we all get stuck in our "inner safe house" also known as a comfort zone. We get too comfortable being around others who aren't positive leaders, we are consumed by negativity, and we can't seem to move forward in our current or past situations. If this is you, you are not alone. All of this was once my comfort zone.

There was a time where I thought, "This is how my life is supposed to be." I'm glad I was wrong. Thank God my life turned out for the better when I thought it was turning for the worse. Despite the pros and cons of being comfortable to a certain extent, if you aren't living the life you always wanted to live, then you must separate yourself from your comfort zone. It's easy to do the daily routines you used to do and stay within the confines of least resistance, but if you want to make progress in your life, you need to break free from what holds you back. To release the items that are hindering you, it is important to be aware what they are. This can include your mindset, the way you deal with your stress, your surroundings, and your emotions. After recognition, the next step is to change anything that will not help you advance in life. A good example of this is your loser type of person. They won't allow you to prosper without putting negativity in your life. Either way, if you know you deserve happiness, don't get comfortable with them and yourself. Sometimes, playing it safe isn't always the best way to go when you are fearful of a new challenge. I want you to become aware that comfort zones aren't healthy if there isn't any growth. I understand, in them we've created a sense of familiarity but when we step outside of our "safe" area, we're taking a risk, and opening ourselves up to numerous possibilities. If I may ask, how else would you learn without taking risks? I don't think you can unless you put yourself out there in uncomfortable situations and explore.

Even though getting out of your comfort zone may be stressful, they aren't necessarily comforting. We form these fearful walls to protect us from any danger of the unknowns. As a result, we feel like we're stuck and can't figure a way out. Keep in the back of your mind, by doing this will close yourself to numerous opportunities of self-development. By you acting fearful will limit your capabilities of moving forward. Again, getting out of your comfort zone is not simple, but this can be done with confidence. It's more than telling yourself, "I want to change. I want to go back to my old happy self." If there is no action behind those words, then you are wasting your breath! I want to encourage you to renew your comfort zone in doing things that make you want to change. Even if you see little growth with your happiness or anything in your life, keep going. Continue to push forward towards the results you are looking for. If you need assistance, refer back to the separation formula. Write down the positive and negative habits and simply, do the math. Believe in yourself and make growth a priority to teach you what you need to learn.

The metamorphosis of a butterfly is formed after the caterpillar is hatched from the cocoon. Just like the caterpillar, we all have formed a cocoon that is designed as protection to keep us in our comfort zone. We have cocoons for our emotions, relationships, jobs, education, and self-environment. At some point in the evolution, the caterpillar is formed into a butterfly and is ready to open the cocoon. In other words, time will reveal when it's ready for you to change. You will figure out what needs to be shifted and be confident in the process but before this is done, you must open your cocoon to become the butterfly you want to be. Remember, anything you want to change can change, if you are willing to separate yourself and spread your wings. Right now, it is your time to stop being a caterpillar, break out of your cocoon and become a butterfly.

Your Healing Process

I conclude that bringing ourselves back into alignment with positivity is a big part of everyone's soul purpose. But some people don't bother with healing themselves until they're presented with an ultimatum by their body, such as feeling sick, anxiety, or severe depression. Realize, our bodies reflect our inner most being. This is potentially a wonderful thing if you're in great shape physically, emotionally, and spiritually. On the other hand, if there is buried pain, discomfort, or negativity inside you, it will at some point manifest into your physical reality. I want to reassure you to think about the way you repair yourself. If you don't have any active coping mechanisms, it is essential for you to separate from the unhealthy healing habits. This will only cause you more internal hurt.

I will like to categorize our negative experiences called wounds. Inside your wound is a scar, which tells a story with a lesson learned. Sadly, some of us don't improve from our experiences. We let them turn us into something we're not promised to be. Because of this we cope by doing drugs, negative gossiping, hang with people who don't add value to our character, we hold in these emotions and so on, as an outlet to manage our stressors. Regardless, we all have unique healing processes to deal with our lives and I'm not judging those who do these types of things. In the same token, if you're honest with yourself, I think you are aware your problems won't fade away by doing anything that is hurting your body or mind. Whatever you feel internally will cause your emotions to be shown.

Let's imagine the last time you had a cut. If you think about the wound, you applied a healing ointment and a Band-Aid. Every now and then, you checked the cut; but as the time passed; you noticed the cut healed. Well just like a physical cut, we can do the same with our scars we carry with us. There is no time length for your healing process, but how you use your time will let you know. You have a choice of a positive or negative coping habit. If you choose positivity, you possess the real Band-Aid you've been looking for to heal yourself. This Band-Aid includes: healthier habits, positivity, positive self-environment and so on. On the other side, if you choose to continue with your negative habits, your wounds will never heal, your problems will continue, and you will still feel the same pain.

It is up to us to study our scars, discover the lesson, and to share them. This is why I'm sharing my story with you because this is a key to healing, by seeing the world from another perspective. Don't ever think there isn't an outlet to your current situation. There is always an answer hidden in every problem. Even though I haven't always seen things clearly, I'm not ashamed of my wounds. I know everything happens for a reason, but I am a lot stronger than I used to be. I have persevered and I'm proud of myself. Now it's your turn to shine.

All in all, be encouraged to learn from your scars or experiences, so you can know what to avoid for the future. Don't ever allow your brokenness decide if you'll restore or not. This is your personal quest of self-discovery towards a newer you. *Nothing But Happiness.*

"The greatest illusion of this world is the illusion of separation. Things you think are separate and different are actually one and the same. We are all one people, but we live as if divided."

Guru Pathik

"One of the keys to happiness is a bad memory."

Rita Mae Brown

"Happiness is like a butterfly. The more you chase it, the more it elude you, but if you turn your attention to other things, it will come and sit quietly on your shoulder."

Henry David Thoreau

"The sooner you step away from your comfort zone; the sooner you'll realize that it really wasn't all that comfortable."

Eddie Harris Jr.

"Pain will come with time, but time will heal the pain."

Anthony Liccione

CHAPTER 4
INSPIRE

In a culture obsessed with vanity, we often overlook the important role of inspiration. Inspiration awakens us to newer possibilities and gives a burst of positive energy. Inspiration propels a person from discouragement to encouragement, unconfident to confident, and transforms the way we perceive our own capabilities. I believe inspiration is the best prescription to ever give to someone. Reason being, inspiration and motivation are the same thing because these are both mind driving forces to make someone want to achieve something. Each one of us are inspired and motivated by different aspects. This is why by using your words, your God-given gift, or your presence is specific to those you can help. It is the key ingredient to give someone lifetime positive results. You have everything inside you to impact them in such a great way.

Let's think about our history from Rosa Parks, Harriet Tubman, Gandhi, Malcolm X, Dr. Martin Luther King Jr., and Muhammed Ali and what inspired these ordinary people to do such extraordinary things. We realize they were selfless, creative, courageous, and just dared to be different. These people are true leaders who believed they could change the world despite the odds and weren't afraid to try. If you aren't inspiring anyone, why can't you have the same mindset as them? What's stopping you to become this type of person and changing the lives of those who need your inspiration?

My Biggest Inspiration

My great-grandmother, Alberta Gramby, is my biggest inspiration, encouraging warrior, and humongous supporter. There aren't enough words to describe this woman but to sum it up; she is inspiring, loving, and caring. She's a strong God-fearing woman who's wise in her years. Throughout her life, she has faced many adversities, but despite this, she remains with a smile on her face. She's the reason why I'll never give up on myself, push through my circumstances, never complain about what I'm going through, and to show love to others.

As I was going through my depression, I wasn't taking my spiritual faith seriously. I did not have a relationship with God, but I knew about him through her teachings and often going to church. She always mentioned to me about her spirituality, which made me wonder why I didn't have one. It was evident to me that it was her faith that has kept her from losing her sanity. At first, I was hesitant about this but she consistently told me, "Having a relationship with God will be the best thing that will ever happen."

On June 6th, 2013 was the day myself, my twin brother, my father, and my great grandmother were all baptized together. It was a special moment for us because I was with the person who inspired me to take my spiritual faith to the next level. I give credit to my great-grandmother because she's the reason I am the person I am today. She has driven me to unimaginable heights, and for that I am forever grateful for her.

Influence is power and the fact that people can use their influence among others shows their strength of personality and character as well. I believe we all have someone who has had a major influence on us. If you're having difficulty discovering your inspirational super power, think of who's your biggest inspiration? What did they say to inspire you? How did they inspire you? Why are they your biggest inspiration?

Other than those courageous stories we've watched on TV, legends told from others, listened on the news, or know those people with brave journeys on how they've overcame their tough circumstances. We're so intrigued by their quest that it makes us forget about our own adventures. Whether you experienced something major or minor, you are someone's motivator because of the story behind you. This makes you a conqueror because each experience you had, you learned and conquered the mission. With the knowledge of these life lessons, you have the ability to inspire someone else going through the same thing. However the problem is, as selfish humans, we don't know who's going through anything. We hold in our feelings, no one can see past the smiles or laughs, and we pretend like everything is "perfect," when it's not. Whether we want to accept it or decline it, we are all hurting and broken. This is why the power of inspiration is important. You have no idea who you can uplift until you put yourself out there. Just as my great grandmother inspires me every day, I believe we all possess this powerful tool. The question is whether you will use this life changing God-given gift or not.

Your God-Given Gift

I have no doubt we all are born with a God-given gift. You may not see it but God put it inside you somewhere. Each one of us is uniquely, remotely designed for a specific gift. When you discover your gift, I want you to realize it is for YOU and only for YOU. In reality, there are a small percentage of people who use their full capacity such as a professional athlete, professional dancer, entrepreneurs, an executive chef, and so on. Meanwhile, there are those of you who hold back your gift, many of you have not yet discovered it, and some of you have not even recognized it's right in front of you. I want you to realize your gift is put inside you to inspire those around you.

You may ask yourself, "What is my God-given gift?" or "How do I discover it?" Well, I like to believe it is something you do perfectly with not much effort. To help you, think about this question: What do you think you do your BEST at naturally? Can you sing? Do you have an eye for photography? Are you a visual learner? Can you cook a five star course meal? Gifts are something you do genuinely, with no effort. To continue, by discovering your God-given gift, it will gear you towards your inspirational powers. You must BELIEVE and have FAITH in this gift in order to see impactful results. Your gift is your strength, which can inspire someone else's weaknesses.

For some odd reason, my passion was and still is to help others. I wasn't aware of this but I attracted to those who needed assistance because it made me feel happy to help them. You could be a stranger to me and if I knew I could help you, I'll be gladly to do it. I would give you money, food, even the clothes on my back if you needed it. By realizing this, has helped me discover my God-Given gift. While it appeared to be based on a desire to help others, the underlying reason for wanting to rescue someone is because they will need us at some point in time. Being that positive person for them has helped me change their own outlook and attitude in life. By doing good deeds and volunteering to assist others has made me feel fulfilled because helping others in need is a rewarding feeling.

Without a doubt, the best feeling in the world is activating someone's happiness. This will make your life more meaningful by seeing their expression. Smiles are contagious, and we should all strive to keep a smile on someone's face and ourselves. Realize that there are people out there who need what you have to offer them. Your words, nurturing care, love, smile, kindness and so on can assist those in need of it. If you aren't a helping hand, you should become one. You can go volunteer your time in your community to serve others, food kitchens, churches, homeless shelters, hospitals, and the list can go on. It doesn't have to be someone you know personally, but help those who require it. It will open your eyes to realize you can make a difference. You have everything inside you to become a positive influence to others. Seeing a smile or even tears of joy makes it all worth it. It's as simple as that.

Discovering and claiming in something you love to do will have an amazing effect on your life. You can provide a contribution to this world because it needs it. When you open yourself up to what you love and makes you feel happy, you will find your purpose.

Your God-Given Purpose

You are here on Earth for a purpose! You were born for a reason. You may have questioned your purpose many times but I believe this answer cannot be found in school, another person, an item, or your current job. This is found digging deep within your inner soul. Once you encounter your God-given gift, this will steer you towards the reason you were born. Bishop T.D Jakes says, "If you can't figure out your purpose, figure out your passion. For your passion will lead you directly to your purpose." Your unique gift is drilled in you on purpose so you can offer it to the world. You are a person who's designed for something far greater than yourself and you are well equipped.

Discovering your purpose isn't the easiest thing to do. The struggle of this is reminding yourself of it on a daily basis and working to the point where you become that purpose. This is a lifetime commitment because living in your purpose will become a daily habit. You'll wake up every day with it on your mind, live your life to the fullest, and chase your passion. You must believe in your aspiration because this is what you're called for in life. I do not believe any human being on this Earth doesn't have a purpose. You were created to make someone's life better, to be their encourager, their motivator, lover and much more. Go after this pursuit and be fearless. When you achieve this, know that you will trigger your happiness.

Throughout my life, I trusted there was purpose behind my challenges. I realized there were no accidents or coincidences in anything I experienced because they happened for a reason. This included with my parents' divorce, depression, lack of self-belief, poor ACT/SAT scores, anger, and my self-negative environment. In the beginning, I was frustrated going through these horrible events. However, currently, I don't live with any regrets. I figured, purpose isn't what you do, but it is how you discover who you truly are. I trusted God and myself to create the person I am today because my purpose is greater than my challenges!

Understanding both your God-Given gift and God-given purpose is essential. Once you recognize them, there are people that you may know who struggle with these aspects. To be successful at helping those around you, it is necessary to install *inspiration* in them. By doing this, will help ignite their flame to continue on in life.

TOUCH

Do you feel like you don't possess enough inspiration to help others? Do you think your story can't help anyone? Do you think your voice doesn't matter? Some people may read this and say yeah that's me. You may think:

"Brandon, I have no idea how to help other people."

"I have no capabilities to inspire myself or others."

"I have no purpose." "I don't know my gift."

"No one will ever listen to what I have to say."

If any of these are your responses, don't feel discouraged. These were once mine too because I felt like I had nothing to offer to anyone. But, I was wrong being inspiration is the reason why I'm writing this book. I have no doubt there is someone out there that is struggling with their happiness and is lost in what to do next. I want to strengthen you by my quest that it is possible to achieve the happiness you are looking for. Remind yourself you do have the ability to encourage someone, but there are a couple of conditions you need to remember before you go out there to inspire other people. The most important aspect is you must have a heart to help others. You cannot uplift someone if you are a know-it-all. Everybody is energized and motivated by different aspects so you can't dive into a situation without prepping yourself first. Your personal narrative of what you've been through or your presence of just listening can be enough inspiration for someone who needs it.

I've realized some people want to be seen and some people want to be heard, but you my friend, have the ability to touch someone. What I mean by this is you will open the gate of communication between yourself and the person you choose to motivate. Here's another acronym to help you build a relationship to inspire someone. This acronym is **TOUCH**.

T is to build *trust* with the person. To inspire other people, they have to have hope in the relationship. No one is going to tell you their story if you don't establish the trust bridge. Building the trust for one another will allow that person to feel that they can be vulnerable and the environment will be safe. Also, don't forget to show genuine feelings towards this person so you know how to encourage them.

O is to *open* your ears to hear their story. You must be an active listener instead of a responder. Some people don't want to hear you speak, rather just listen to them. If you establish a conversation, they should be doing most of the talking, not you.

Open your mind to what you are about to hear because remember, not everyone experiences the same situations you do. However, show empathy, do not judge, and ask questions to let them know you care. You want them to know you are a reliable person.

U is to be **upfront** about the advice you are about to give to the person. You must be honest with yourself and with the people you want to inspire. They need to see the real you, not a person who "pretends" that they care. Be honest with your story, your questions, and the advice you give. I suggest to never give them any recommendation, if you don't follow it for yourself. You should present them relatable advice on where you're coming from. Additionally, be careful with the choice of words you use for advice. People need constructive criticism but not in a harmful way. By using encouraging words will make them feel safe to express themselves. Be optimistic to uplift their energy and make sure it's proper judgement to their personal experience. You are entitled to your own opinion but make sure it's what they need to be reassured on. I have found that much of the time they know the right thing to do; they just need someone to confirm it for them. Either way, as long as your words are genuine and your presence helps, that's all that matters.

C is showing that person you **care**. You have to be vulnerable to the person you want to inspire. Put yourself in their shoes to try to understand what they are going through. If you have similar stories, it should be that much easier to have a heart to heart conversation with them. If they see how you went through your struggles, it will boost their motivation to attack theirs. If you can't understand their story, it doesn't hurt to ask questions to get a better understanding. To repeat, not everyone goes through the same circumstances so you can inquire about what they've been through in more detail. This will show you're concerned about them, which is a sign you care.

H is for *helping others* which will activate your inspirational power. I believe assisting can come in numerous forms but this should be given to another person without any reasoning. There is an importance of serving others because everyone needs some type of help at some point in their lives. However many times, we need a reason to help someone because they did something for us. I'm not saying looking for a return favor is wrong but you should help someone without expecting anything back. You have the ability to save someone and people will never forget what you've done for them.

To play devil's advocate, most of the times, we all have to do things for ourselves first before helping others. We must heal, love, support, encourage, and trust ourselves to believe everything will be okay. Once this process is done, believe me, it'll be your time to inspire other people. Don't be discouraged if the people you inspire don't want to change. Again, many people are "comfortable" where they are in life and you do not have a responsibility to change them. Your purpose of inspiration is to plant the seed. Let God and time take care of the rest. *Nothing But Happiness.*

"One smile can start a friendship. One word can end a fight. One look can save a relationship. One person can change your life."

Anonymous

"You have two hands, one for helping yourself, the other for helping others."

Audrey Hepburn

"When you realize God's purpose for your life isn't just about you, he will use you in a mighty way."

Dr. Tony Evans

"Your mission, your purpose, and your destiny will all be tied to one thing-your gift."

Steve Harvey

"Whether you experienced something major or minor, you are someone's motivator because of the story behind you."

Brandon King

CHAPTER 5

HAPPY

I wish happiness was found under a rock, something we can purchase in the store, a subject that is taught in school, or a prize we can win in a game. Unfortunately, any of these options aren't the case. The good news is if you aren't experiencing this emotion, you have the ability to feel it right now. There isn't any formula to have "perfect happiness" and to live every day perfectly, but you are programmed to feel happiness. It's the mistakes, the people, obstacles, or ourselves that we allow to alter this emotion. Despite this, today I encourage you to take action towards this achievement.

As you read so far, you've witnessed the adventure I've gone through. Today if someone asked me, "Brandon, how happy are you right now?" I would respond, "I'm not happy, I'm content." In other words, I realized happiness comes when you feel satisfied and fulfilled. Being content is not about denying your negative emotions, or pretending to feel joy all the time. It is a feeling of contentment that life is just as it should be. If I could go back, I wouldn't change anything! I never felt bad for myself because there wouldn't be any room for happiness. There's no need to complain because I'm stronger from the pain. I have valuable lessons to bring forth with me and I will appreciate what life has taught me thus far.

I want to refresh your memory on the steps I've taken to achieve the happiness. Again, these are there for encouragement.

First, transform your mind to discipline the negative emotions because thinking and speaking positively will produce healthier habits. Next, concentrate on the important things in life that keeps you happy. Focus and prioritize on what's important on your plate and acknowledge, accept, and act upon changing your inner feelings. Separate yourself from anything that doesn't serve you positivity or happiness. This includes negativity, negative people, and the negative healing habits you have. Discover your God-given gift and purpose to inspire yourself and others around you. As a result, when you apply all of these steps, you'll realize you're in control of your happiness. You'll be strong enough to neglect any person, experience, or environment that makes you feel unhappy, or takes the happiness away. You must believe in yourself and your definition of what happiness means to you. Then you will be much more effective at reaching the kind of world you are destined to have.

Believe in Your Definition

Nowadays, one of the most common problems with individuals is that they do not believe in themselves. Many of you constantly doubt if your happiness will come back, your God-given gifts/purpose, emotions, and other numerous aspects that make you who you truly are. By doing this causes you to overthink your capabilities, which makes you waste precious time. If you are looking to improve yourself, your life, and the way others view you, you have to understand the importance of believing in yourself. If you miss this opportunity of accomplishing this very important goal, you will continue to question yourself all throughout your life.

I had to believe that my happiness was inside of me. I knew it was in there, I just needed help pulling it out. Since it revolved around my parents' marriage, it was tough for me to have faith it was there. I couldn't imagine myself being happy because I thought they were in control of it. Overtime, I had to understand this was false. I am responsible for my own happiness; no one else, not even my parents. Now I know, I can't revolve anything that can be stolen from me. For those who did not know this, learn from my mistake. I trust everyone has some type of definition of what happiness is, but it does not orbit around a person, place, memory, or anything that can be taken away. Happiness has no stop signs, bridges, sidewalks, or checkpoints. It is a continuous road of contentment. The most important thing about creating your interpretation is that it must be your definition. When you think of this idea, it must fit you, and only you. Once, you detail of what happiness means to you, it will put you in a better position to identify the necessary steps required to get there. And when you get there, you must live by your definition because nothing can make you unhappy, despite the difficulties and challenges you may face. Take it day by day and continue to enjoy the process of the present moments.

Get the picture of when you believe in your abilities, skills, talents, and values; you will develop a new logic to yourself and your life. The more you believe, the more you will become energized to accomplish whatever you desire. By using your

God-given gift, believing in your God-given purpose, and applying all your capabilities to your fullest potential, it can produce powerful results in yourself, your loved ones, communities, and at your job. I promise when you start believing in yourself, you will feel unstoppable. If you ever catch yourself doubting, realize how far you have come. Even if you can't "feel" the happiness, just know that it is inside of you. I'll even suggest getting in touch with all the corky, silly things that make you smile. It's funny because we have our own joyful happiness support system inside of us. You just have to trust yourself to know your happiness is right around the corner but you need to be patient. If you have trouble with this word like I did, maybe this is something to start practicing instead of getting frustrated.

Celebrate Your Patience

If you haven't noticed, we live in an "instant gratification" society. We're all equally condemned of wanting something at a short notice, or sooner rather than later, at one point. It seems to be waiting for something, isn't worth the wait anymore. But we all understand that great things take time. On the other hand, great things will not come our way, if we do not know how to be submissive. This is why by celebrating your patience is far better than having whatever you wish for at the snap of a finger. The ability to teach yourself to wait will make you become more grateful.

Nowadays, being patient is tough due to our impatient norms. Since we live in a world where no one knows how to be patient (thanks to social media) we've become instant gratification people. Instant gratification is an impatient person who wants something when they want it. If this person doesn't get their desires or wants met, this makes them become tense, anxious, or unfulfilled. If I am describing you, this doesn't make you a horrible person. Not too long ago, this was me. Back then, I hated going through my parents' divorce. To cope with my frustration, I had two difficult patient challenges. One being my favorite hobby was to shop and the process of attending a community college. At the time, I couldn't control my soft addiction impulses because it took my mind off the negative emotions. I thought because I had this temporary excitement of buying the latest Jordan's or wore the coolest outfit, it made me feel happy. Then, later on the joy faded away so I continued on with this habit. I was running in this cycle of repeating this short term confusion because I wanted to hide my feelings than face my reality.

While I was going through this shopping phase, I was spending money like I had a million dollars. Meanwhile, I had to prepare myself to attend County College of Morris due to poor SAT/ACT scores. The good thing about this school is the affordable tuition so I was happy about that. But truthfully, I was upset because this wasn't the school I wanted to go to. After graduation, all of my friends attended real colleges so it made me feel like a loser. Then again, I had no ambition of what I wanted to do with my life. I had no type of direction of any careers to pursue. With that, just like any clueless teenager who doesn't know what to do, I started out as a Liberal Arts and Humanities major. I had this major for about a year and none of the classes I took gave me excitement. My patience was running low so I went to see my advisor. She suggested I take a class called Career Development to gear me towards my career goals. I agreed to take the class so I registered immediately. In a nutshell, the class taught me exactly what I needed to know to pursue a different career choice. After the following semester, I switched my major to Exercise Science to pursue a career in health and wellness.

I approached the second year in County College of Morris and I realized I had to get serious about my future. Usually community college students are done in two years and I was nowhere near finished with my curriculum. This made me nervous and impatient with myself. I tried to figure out if I could graduate by the end of the spring semester next year along with my brother who also attended CCM. Unfortunately, it would have taken me another year to graduate and I didn't want to be left behind. Throughout the year, I started to work harder and finally, I accumulated enough credits to start the transfer process.

Thinking about attempting to reapply to my dream school, Montclair State University gave me chills. My guidance counselor's words were stuck in my head and I knew I had to send my worthless SAT/ACT scores again. The night I went to apply, I felt knots in my throat. As I was typing in the school's website in the search engine, my fingers kept shaking. All of the sudden, as I arrived to the home page website, I saw in bold letters, *"Montclair State University will no longer require SAT scores."* My jaw dropped. I couldn't believe the one thing that affected my acceptance, didn't matter anymore. I was so happy that this burden was lifted off of me. After this, my whole perspective of applying to this school changed. I started to build confidence because I didn't have to worry about my SAT scores. This gave me better focus to put more time and effort in the personal statement. By the time I submitted my statement, I was more hopeful in myself. I just had a good feeling about getting an acceptance letter from Montclair State.

As weeks went by, my hard work paid off and I received my acceptance letter to Montclair State University as a transfer student. This was the happiest day of my life. In that moment, I wanted to run to my high school to shove the letter in my guidance counselor's face. Unfortunately, I did not do this, but it didn't matter. I proved to myself that I could get into this school. I thanked God because he allowed this door to open for me. Everything I've been through with this college process taught me, every aspect in life takes patience, even happiness.

It took some time to grasp, patience has its numerous benefits. I changed my ungrateful and unappreciative attitude by becoming a person of delayed gratification. I realized, by having some areas in my life held up, made me become grateful when it came to pass. True happiness takes patience and consistent effort. If we don't have this discipline, we'll continue to search for instant gratifying moments which can become addictive, if not controlled. We all deserve everything we're looking for, but we need to celebrate what we have now, that way when we get what we want, it'll be even better! Remember, anything worth having is worth the wait. Just don't ever give up on yourself. Even if you don't see the light at the end of the tunnel, DON'T GIVE UP. Even if you feel like you have no strength left in you, DON'T GIVE UP. Even if you feel like you've hit rock bottom, DON'T GIVE UP.

If I Can, You Can

There was a point in my life where I was searching for someone to make me happy, inspire me, motivate me, believe in me, and encourage me. I was searching and searching everywhere. I couldn't find anything and I wanted to give up. Then I recognized, I had to become this person. Through this renewal, I had to realize all of these voids are necessary to have within. I couldn't depend on any person to help me with this because it was an inside job. For those of you who search for these things, I strengthen you to take a deep look within yourself. You have what it takes to fulfill the voids you seek. It's a matter of changing your choice of words from, "I can't" to "I can." It's not straightforward, but keep reminding yourself, "I can love myself"... "I can inspire myself"... "I believe in myself" and so on. These should be your daily reminders but it's more than just words. You must recognize you have to really believe in what you speak to yourself and work hard during this evolution. You will always listen to yourself first and your daily commitment is necessary because anything worth having requires a process. If I can achieve this, I know you can too!

The question isn't how not to give up, it's why you shouldn't give up. Throwing in the towel each time you experience something negative isn't what you want to do. I could have given up on myself for allowing my parents' divorce turn my emotions into anger. But I realized quitting will get you nowhere and will become a habit, if it is not controlled in advance. The best thing you can say to yourself is, "At least I gave it a shot" or "At least I know better for the future." As I believe everyday should be a happy day, it should also be a learning day. Learn by jumping into those tasks you think you cannot achieve. Challenge yourself and give your best effort at every opportunity that you come across. Make a promise to yourself that you won't give up trying, no matter what the outcome is. This is your learning process because you are at least attempting something. Just believe you can succeed in any experience you face because you are more than a conqueror. You are a lot stronger than you think and what others may see. Lastly, don't let a minor obstacle stop you from achieving your happiness. You deserve to be happy! I vow, true happiness belongs to those who master the art of molding their lives into something greater than regretting their past. Keep that mindset and never give up until you reach your destination.

In life, I figured there's always a chance to grow. From my struggle, the pain, the realness of my reality, made me become humble from my experiences. These obstacles were put there to build my self-belief which made me never give up. Life isn't about living in regrets, but it's about self-awareness. I know mistakes, disappointments, and stress are going to happen, but my future is bright! Each day I'm learning and building my legacy. Now it's your turn to discover who you are and make a difference.

Your Self-Discovery and Legacy

Whether we want it to happen, this life we are living will soon end. When you look back at your life, you want to be remembered by what you gave to a single person, your community, loved ones, and so on. A legacy isn't only about leaving what you earned, but also what you learned. Do you want to be remembered by your passion, your uniqueness, your kindness to others, or your inspirational powers? It could be tons of ideas, but leaving a legacy is essential of our life's work. You should take advantage of the opportunity to make an impact in this world now. Just remember what's important to you and remember to create your mark in yourself, your loved ones, communities, jobs, and so on. You will realize what you leave behind will benefit those after your generation.

Each day, I want to leave a legacy by making a difference in someone else's life. Too often we underestimate the power of TOUCH, a helping hand, being a positive role model, smiling, all of which has the potential to turn someone's life around. I hope what I went through in my life is as inspiring to those who need it. This self-discovery has taught me, the tougher the lesson, the bigger the blessing. I am a witness you can really achieve anything! My message to you is this is just the beginning of your race. Take the daily action steps, put your mind to your dreams, and run towards them. Tomorrow is never guaranteed so I take the time to be thankful for everything I have. Now it's time to look forward to what the future holds. Through it all, I know I have every reason in the world to be happy!

Life is a story. Each day, we all start with a blank page. By creating your path, don't forget to leave your footprints on the pages. These are what you want to be remembered by in your legacy. Within this legacy, we all will make a discovery of some sort, inside our mind, soul, our heart, and purpose. You find out who you are meant to be, and what you want in life. Just remember to always be true to you. The only person you have to prove right or wrong is yourself. With that being said, no matter how accomplished you are, how many friends envy you, how many people doubt you, if you aren't happy within your heart, nothing else will matter in life. You have to encounter your own worth and make sure you push yourself daily. Value and challenge yourself to be greater than you were before you read this book. Learn what personal qualities are important to you, makes you upset, how to communicate your feelings, acknowledge your flaws, and celebrate your successes. Let go of your anger, regrets, and fears. Be encouraged to love, trust, inspire yourself, your communities, your enemies, and your loved ones. Share your story, have confidence in your mistakes, and don't let anyone else write your journey. Remember, no one can judge your story if they haven't read through the pages of your life. It's up to you to decide how your story finishes. You're responsible for your one life and you will always be important in this world. Finally, don't let NOTHING stop you from being happy! I want to thank you for taking the time to read this book. I hope your spirit is encouraged to continue this fight towards your happiness. You can do this! God Bless you. *Nothing But Happiness.*

"Best thing I ever did was believe in me."
Anonymous

"There is no challenge more challenging than the challenge to improve yourself."
Anonymous

"Happiness comes when you believe in what you are doing, know what you are doing, and love what you are doing."
Brian Tracy

"Patience is the key to happiness."
Imam Ali

"Good things come to those who believe, better things come to those who are patient and the best things come to those who don't give up."
Anonymous

Thank you

This page is dedicated to everyone who has been my support team from the beginning. You guys know who you are. Thank you for the love, encouragement, prayers, support, inspiration, and motivation I need in my life. Most importantly, I thank God for being the head of my life because with him I know all things are possible. Thank you all from the bottom of my heart! To my family, I love you dearly. #NothingButHappiness #GodisGreat

Love,

Brandon

References

Cambridge Dictionaries

About the Author

My name is Brandon King and I'm the author of *Nothing But Happiness*. I'm 23 years old from Morristown, NJ. If you would like to contact me, please email me at nothingbuthappinesss@gmail.com. I would love to hear from you!

Queen

I have named you queen.
There are taller ones than you, taller.
There are purer ones than you, purer.
There are lovelier than you, lovelier,
But you are the queen.